Built By Hand

Written by Max Greenslade

Flying Start
to Literacy®

Contents

Introduction

Long ago, before the machines of today were invented, people built everything they needed using simple tools. They used tools such as hammers and materials such as mud and stone to build things.

Many of the things that were built by
people were huge. It took many, many
people to build them.

Some of these buildings have survived for
thousands of years. Some are the greatest
that have ever been made.

Chapter 1
The biggest pyramid

Pyramids were built thousands of years ago. People built them by stacking millions of stones into a pyramid shape. Some of these pyramids are very big.

Pyramid of Khafra in Egypt

The Pyramid of Khafra (*kar-fra*)
is as tall as a 47-storey building.
Its base is as big as 110 basketball courts.

But it is not the biggest pyramid
in the world.

Great Pyramid of Khufu in Egypt

The Great Pyramid of Khufu (*koo-foo*)
is even bigger. It contains more than
two million stones and is as tall as a
48-storey building. Its base is as big as
120 basketball courts.

It is the tallest pyramid in the world
but it is not the biggest pyramid.

Great Pyramid of Cholula in Mexico

The biggest pyramid in the world is the Great Pyramid of Cholula (*cho-loo-la*). This pyramid is only as tall as a 22-storey building, but its base is bigger than 480 basketball courts. This pyramid took 1500 years to build. It is so big, it looks like a hill.

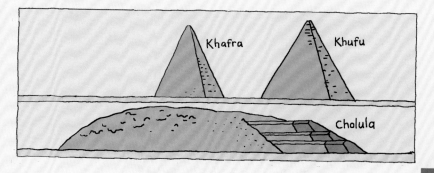

Chapter 2

The heaviest stone ever moved

Huge stones were used to make buildings and statues. Often these stones came from places far away.

Long ago, people dragged these stones to the building before lifting them into place. These stones were very heavy and difficult to move and lift.

Herod's Temple in Jerusalem

Herod's Temple was built with large stone bricks. The heaviest of these bricks weighed the same as 38 trucks.

But these are not the heaviest stones ever moved.

Jupiter Temple in Lebanon

The Jupiter Temple is made from stones.
Each stone weighs as much as 48 trucks.

But these are not the heaviest stones
ever moved.

Statue of Ramses in Egypt

The heaviest stone ever moved was used to make the statue of Ramses (*ram-seez*). Ramses was a king in ancient Egypt.

The statue was carved from a single piece of stone. This stone weighed nearly as much as 77 trucks.

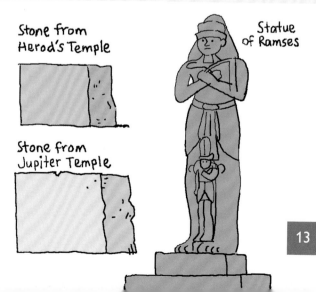

Stone from Herod's Temple

Stone from Jupiter Temple

Statue of Ramses

Chapter 3
The biggest mud-brick building

Some of the oldest buildings in the world are made of mud bricks. People stacked the mud bricks together and covered them with mud paste to give a smooth finish.

Shibam skyscrapers in Yemen

The tallest mud buildings in the world are in a city called Shibam (*she-bam*). Some of these buildings are 13 storeys tall and some are more than 500 years old.

But these are not the biggest mud-brick buildings in the world.

15

Bam Castle in Iran

Bam Castle was the biggest mud-brick building in the world until an earthquake destroyed most of it in 2003. This castle covered an area as big as 428 basketball courts. It was 2000 years old when it was destroyed.

So what is the biggest mud-brick building now?

Great Mosque of Djenné in Africa

The biggest mud-brick building in the world
is the Great Mosque of Djenné (*mosk of jen-ay*)
in Africa. It is as big as 13 basketball courts.
The main hall can hold nearly 3000 people
and the walls are nearly one metre thick.
Every year a team of 80 builders covers the
mosque in mud to preserve it.

Chapter 4
The longest wall

People build walls to keep their enemies out and to separate people from each other. Sometimes these walls are very long and many that exist today are thousands of years old.

What is the longest wall in the world?

Walled fortress in India

This fortress has a stone wall surrounding it that is 36 kilometres long. In some parts the walls are seven metres thick.

This is a long wall but it is not the longest wall.

Hadrian's Wall in north England

Hadrian's Wall is more than 70 kilometres long. It was built nearly 2000 years ago and it only took six years to build.

But it is not the longest wall in the world.

The Great Wall of China

The longest wall ever built is the Great Wall of China. It is more than 6700 kilometres long. Some parts of the wall are more than seven metres tall and five metres thick. The wall is made of stone, mud, wood and dirt.

Millions of workers took more than 1000 years to build the wall.

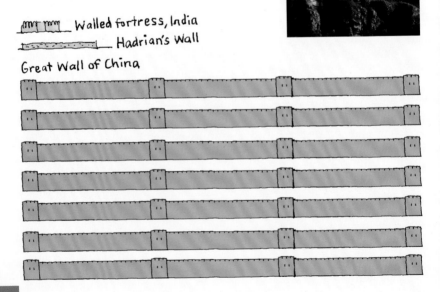

Walled fortress, India

Hadrian's Wall

Great Wall of China

How big is it?

Great Pyramid of Cholula
Its base is 550 metres by
450 metres and it is
66 metres tall.

Mosque of Djenné
Built on a platform that is
75 metres by 75 metres, with
walls up to 15 metres tall.

Statue of Ramses
Made from a single
stone that weighed
1000 tonnes.

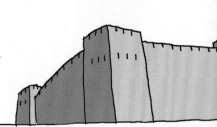

Great Wall of China
6700 kilometres long.